HOW TO INCREASE YOUR HAPPINESS!

BY

OCHEI INNOCENT

DEDICATION

TO ALL,

WHO NEVER

FROWN!

CHAPTER ONE

HER HUSBAND LET HER DOWN

Armed robbers went to a man's house in a city in Anambah Nigeria. He was a man of great wealth but the robbers took away everything.

The Rock's waited for an opportunity to shoot him but he did not offer any resistance.

And so they took away everything belonging to him and expected him to cry or make noise but the man did not of the above

So the tips became worried. They have gone about 100 m from his place when their leaders said to the others let us go back and find out why this man did not raise his voice and did not abuse us as many other persons would do

Instead this man let us take away as many things as we wanted. Something must be terribly wrong and we need to find out so that the gods will not attack us even after we have made some attachments.

So he and his evil accomplices they turned around and went back.

They met the man and his family praying giving thanks to God that their lives were spared.

So they asked the people why you are rejoicing when such great calamity has befallen you.

They reply they got shocked them. They were told that they can take away the material properties but that they cannot even ever take away your joy. They asked again and received again the same answer.

Worried by his conscience the leader of the team said they should return everything to the man. However the man said no that they should take everything away because don't they took his material possessions they did not take away what he valued most and which was his happiness.

It turned out to be that the teens were actually still in because they believed that material possessions can bring you happiness. They fail to realize that the rich also cry and that demons trouble both the rich and the poor. Therefore immense happiness cannot consist of his material possession.

Here is another story that should interest all of us. It is about a jealous housewife that thought her happiness depended on the attention or not given to her by her husband.

Sooner than later she found out that her husband was to <u>timing. In</u> simple language or in plain language her husband was seeing another woman.

Because she applied her happiness to whatsoever her husband can do or not do she became very angry and indeed sad. So when she was about to wash the husband's clothes, she found in his trouser pocket, the address and telephone number of a woman.

Of course she placed a call to the woman and it turned out to be that the woman on the other side was not pretentious.

She told the woman what she did not want to hear and the truth of what she was: a concubine to her husband.

Our friend was so sad and jealous that she began to monitor her husband's documents for hints and things that need to be hidden.

It did not take long for her to find the concubine's receipts in her husband's pocket. It turned out to be that the woman [the concubine] had been sick and the husband had taken her to a hospital. The receipt she got was the receipt with which the concubine was once treated.

Unfortunately for this woman, she has been asking her husband for money for over a decade and her husband always claimed not to have money!

Already inflamed by her jealousy and bitterness she became very sad and decided to take action but the action she took surprised everybody.

She went to the same hospital and confessed to the doctor that she was not sick but needed to be treated with the same remedies that the concubine had though the concubine was sick and she was not.

The doctor having listened to her, knew that something was very wrong with her. How can anyone out of jealousy request to receive the same medical treatment as a concubine just to get back at her cheating husband?

When a woman ties her happiness to what the husband does or does not do, she can do anything when disappointed. So this lady went to the hospital and asked to be injected and given all the necessary treatments received by the other woman and so the medical doctor of life's her.

Out of jealousy, she wanted the cheating husband to waste two hundred percent of what he spent before since he could afford to keep two women! She did not care about the pains she would get with each injection. Not to talk of the danger of wrong prescription, etc.

However instead of medicines the doctor connived with the nurses and they were pumping the angry woman with ordinary water! She also wanted to feel pain like the other woman hoping that as she groaned in pain, her husband would feel for her. Unknown to her, the doctor had let her husband into her secret pans for they were school buddies!

And after three days she was discharged from the hospital. She went home.

Only when she got home did she realize that her husband had so many other concubines. Knowing that his wife had discovered his secret, he decided to let her into the full story by dropping other "hints" or evidences round the house where she would see them. Also, the husband was unrepentant. He continued to see that concubine thus, increasing the wife's sadness.

Should your happiness be tied to what a person can do or what that person refuses to do?

CHAPTER TWO

MATERIAL POSSESSIONS?

Number one is that your happiness is not in material possessions. There is no material possession that can make a man happy. The human mind has been so attuned ignorantly into thinking that when you own every material thing on earth, you will be very happy.

That is very far from the truth. The heart of man is like a graveyard and the grave is insatiable. The more people die every day, the more the mouth of the grave is open to receive more people. The heart of man I repeat is insatiable.

Many rich and great men have since discovered that their happiness does not depend on material possession.

Alexander the Great was so disappointed by the inability of his material possessions to make him happy to the extent that when he died he asked that his arms be put outside the coffin so that people can see that as he was going to heaven he took nothing along to heaven. He then confessed to the medical doctors that attended to him that material possessions do not give happiness.

Many of us are under the illusion that it is when we have money that we will be very happy. That indeed is a great error.

When men have money something else becomes their problem. Look closely at all the billionaires we have. They keep on looking for one new project or the other to undertake. None of them have come up ever to say I am so sorry: I have made enough money and now I want to retire and just be happy! No!

Instead, they keep acquiring more and more wealth! Even the new acquisitions have not given them happiness either!

According to a story told to us by a person from the Middle East: one day a man left his house in search of money or what can give money. He went right around the whole world searching but he was not able to find anybody with anything or formula that could give him instant and sustainable wealth.

Determined, he carried his search from one end of the world to the other until one day he met a man called Santana Goswami.

Those who lived near this man called Santana told our searcher that Santana had something that will give him money.

So our man rushed off to this place and on reaching there he was grossly surprised to see the man they said had the thing that can give somebody money sitting on the floor.

Anyway, he did not go there to rebuke or approve of the man's conduct. He went there to ask for that thing that will give him her money because he believed that money is the only thing that could make him happy. So he decided to be focused and concern himself with only things that concerned his mission!

 Approaching with all fear and humility he asked the man for that thing which could give him money.

The man asked him to go and check in the dustbin that he will find it in the dustbin!

Our friend was shocked to the bone marrow. He asked his host how anyone could have such a wonderful thing and keeps it not in the bank: not in the walls of great institutions but right in the dustbin where useless things are kept and why would a man want to give it so freely to him!

So many questions passed through the mind of the man but he did not have an answer for them.

Since his purpose was to get that thing which could give money he quickly asked for it. He was not the type to beat about the bush so he went straight and requested for what he came for and the host gladly pointed at the dustbin.

So our friend went over and picked it up
and thereafter began his return journey
back to his home.

As he was going home, people heard the
rumor that he had received that in which
could turn everything into gold. So they
began to bring out their pots and pans
for him to turn to gold. Of course since
he himself had received freely he began
to turn the pots and pans of the people
freely into gold.

Hardly had he done this for an hour,
than his hands began to eke him badly.
By the end of two hours, he was so
troubled that he decided to give up the
use of the thing that he found in the
dustbin. Within so short a time, it had
brought him so many problems.

He was so sick and tired that he ended
up in the hospital. While there he had
time to reflect and could see that his

happiness could not have been found in material things.

Many of us today still make the same mistake as this man initially made before retracing his legs.

CHAPTER THREE

WINNING BATTLES?

Secondly, Your happiness is certainly not in conquest. Many a king or invader have left their homes and known to the unknown places to kill and to take what does not belong to them. Some have been under the wrong impression that when they conquer the whole world they will be very happy but history is not on their side.

Most war mongers easily get tired of fighting. Some thought that fighting and conquering people of other nations will make them happy but even after conquering half the world they feel sad and tired. Some even found that while they were away fighting abroad, the home front was parceling a lot of bitterness and concern to them to the extent that they start regretting going out at all.

Conquests do not make one happy.

There was a certain boxer a heavyweight champion. He conquered everybody in his weight category until there were no more opponents for him in that category. To fight any other unbeaten champion, he would have to lose weight and compete in a lower division.

So he became sad. Conquering everybody there was to conquer did not bring him happiness. Instead, it created more problems for him because since he could not get opponents, he could not fight and since he did not fight, he was not paid and his bills began to pile up!

Though, an undisputed champion of the whole world, he was a sad man.

Many wrongly think that happiness can be found by running many races and winning them but the truth remains that many a champion has committed suicide in the end because winning and winning in itself does not translate into happiness.

CHAPTER FOUR

DOES POWER GIVE HAPPINESS?

A politician in Nigeria once complained that before he went into government, he would give free money to his relatives, small amounts that is, and he would get a long thank you.

However, since he went into government, should he give anyone even double of what he used to give, he would spy them hissing and raining curses on him for being stingy. They just believe that once you are in power, the country's cash reserves are yours to plunder.

The above is just one of the problems associated with power.

Once you start pursuing power, your challenges increase. Many will put demands on your finances with promises to do campaign here and there but once your money enters their hands, they disappear into thin air. Thus, making you very sad!

Once you start pursuing power, you get involved in countless meetings that keep you away from your primary sources of income and you know what that means.

Not just that, pursuit of power keeps you away from your family and before you know it, some of your children might derail.

Julius Caesar was a roman general and great politician. He died of political intrigues that led the country to civil war. He was back stabbed by his best friends and stabbed physically by his very best friend Brutus! Can you imagine all the sadness he must have felt at that moment when he uttered the last word that came from his mouth as he fell:

"And you too Brutus?"

If power brings happiness, then why would so many persons in power commit suicide? I did an online search on this and I found that in every generation, there have been countless politicians who took their own life out of frustration.

Under the title: **"Royalty who committed suicide"** Wikipedia listed a large number of such casualties, giving some details on them. You can check it out please.

You can also check out:

"List of heads of state and government who committed suicide."

You will see that having power did not make tens and hundreds of former heads of state happy.

Happiness is made of sterner stuff than either being born into power or having power thrust on you.

To increase your happiness, you do not need to be in power. We go into politics to serve and most times the people we serve turn out to be in-grates!

Most times, leaders are misunderstood and abused until many years after they have died. It is then that the benefits of their good deeds manifest to the understanding of the average man on the street.

A wise man would therefore not put his confidence in pursuit of power.

In the next chapter, I am going to lead us into taking a dispassionate look at what happiness really is and how we can have it and have it abundantly.

CHAPTER FIVE

BY THE WAY, WHAT IS HAPPINESS?

Happiness is your decision. It is what you allow to happen to you after something negative has happened.

You are the one to decide whether you will be sad or you will be happy. No outside can make you sad. You and you alone will take that decision.

Happiness is a decision you make. You resolve and say to yourself that no matter what somebody else has to say about you, you are not going to be sad. People have the right to run their mouths in any direction and manner they want. That is their business.

In fact you can decide well ahead of time that you will not be moved or touched by anything anybody will say. You might want to remind yourself that no matter what you do to please people they will always have one thing or the other to say. You cannot please everybody.

Remember that there is freedom of speech and people are free to say anything they like about you. Even when you take them to court, they go to the court and say well that is my personal opinion of you. The court will not jail them because they are entitled to their personal opinion.

So why would you allow what people have to say to affect you or what they have to do?

Just as you have to decide well ahead of time that whatever your wife or husband does will not have any effect on you, so too should you feel when they say things you do not like. Do as if nothing is happening. That is the best way you treat whatever they say!

Archbishop Benson Idahosa used to say that if you listen too much to what people have to say you will not be able to hear what God is saying to you!

CHAPTER SIX

WHAT IS YOUR ATTITUDE?

Happiness is your attitude to the things that happen around you.

Your attitude in turn is determined by how you see things. If you see only the negative aspects of things you will continue to be sad. But if you can open your eyes to the positive side of every event or activity you will hardly have any reason to be sad.

There is nothing under the sun. There is nothing that happens that does not have a positive side. It is only people with a very negative mind that see only the negative side. They too are the ones that wear frowns everyday!

I remember when we were in secondary school and we left the school compound without any form of authorization from the school authorities. Of course, we were caught outside the school compound at odd hours by the Vice Principal of the school.

When we faced the disciplinary panel, we admitted guilt and they decided to give us a light punishment but it was one that I can never forget all my life.

We were made to write and fill an 80-leaves notebook with the following sentence:

"Mishaps are like knives which I deserve us or cut us".

Normally this is a sentence that will not fill more than a line. There we were with a notebook of at least one hundred and sixty pages, being asked to fill each line with those words.

Needless to say that it took us hours and hours on end before we could fill the notebook in our own handwriting.

The punishment achieved one thing in us: It enabled us to internalize the message of the sentence. For me I got to know that anything that happens and we think is very bad, has its positive side. Even something as negative as a knife which can kill can also be used to build up lives and to protect lives.

 So every event and activity in life is comparable to a two-edged sword. All, with good and bad sides! To keep happy, I look for the positive side and relate with it to protect my sanity.

That event can be a blessing or a curse depending on your attitude and how you see things.

If you want to be happy in life you must not look at things with a pair of negative spectacles. Your prism must see everybody as children of God with positive sides and you will always be looking out for that positive side to relate with. That is the only way you can relate with people successfully.

When you look at life continually from a negative perspective, you will always read meanings into what people are doing and you will always assume that you are under attack whereas the people do not even know that you exist.

CHAPTER SEVEN

WHAT ARE YOU THINKING?

Happiness is what you think in your heart. The bible says that as a man thinks in his heart so he is.

Think evil of no man or woman. Just relate with people, giving trust and without doubt.

Why not be like salt that is without bias? Salt goes every where it is invited!

Happiness is like salt. Wherever salt goes to instead of being dominated it dominates the environment. It changes the taste of everything it comes in contact with.

I think of myself as salt. Wherever I go I sweeten life. Nothing bad embitters the salt. Rather the salt will make it tasty.

Even when salt is overwhelmed, it does not change. Instead it's sinks to the bottom and remains there until what overwhelms it is removed. If you want to get what I mean take salt a spoon of salt and put in a glass of water then increase the water by another glass. You will notice that it will get to a stage where you might not see the salt again. We can safely say at that point that the salt is overwhelmed. As the head of salt, figuratively speaking, is bowed and bloodied but not defeated!

Instead the salt wills I lie low for a while but before you know it, they will come and remove the water by heating or by drying or whatever until only salt will remain at the bottom. Wherever salt goes it sweetens. Salt does not allow the environment to change it from what it is to another thing.

That is why I see myself as salt and I do not allow anything that happens around me, even the ones that seem to over whelm me, to affect me.

Why not be a salt in life?

 Jesus Christ describes Christians as the salts of the Earth.

So I try to understand what salt is. I try to identify the characteristics and qualities of salt. I found among other things that salt has neither nose nor ear! So it can hear nothing and smell nothing. That is why it can go into the kitchen mingle with onions and other things and still retain its taste. That is why it can also go into the toilet mingle with whatever we deposit there and still retain its scent!

So I ask again: why not be salt and remain positive, no matter where you go, whom you meet or what happens?

QUOTE

"The happiness of your life depends upon the quality of your thoughts: therefore, guard accordingly, and take care that you entertain no notions unsuitable to virtue and reasonable nature."

Marcus Aurelius

CHAPTER EIGHT

DO NOT COUNT OFFENCE

Happiness is forgiveness. I want to emphasize the fact that happiness is forgiving people even before they give the offence.

This is certainly something everyone can practice. We need to start today and to do it regularly. I am talking about forgiving offences that people are yet to commit. Not allowing anything anybody can do or say to offend us to the extent that will become bitter. We might be disappointed: that is natural.

It should end too. In fact, for me when I'm relating with fellow human beings I keep remembering that to err is human and to forgive is divine. I keep remembering that the Bible asks me: why not allow myself to be cheated? So I prepare in advance just in case this should happen.

Though I keep praying against such a thing all the time, at the same time I prepare my mind in advance so that when man disappoints or fails me, I will not be totally taken unawares.

Man, we are told, is made from dust or sand and as such, easily blown where it will. Not all men have integrity. Not all men will say something and do it. Anyone that puts his trust in the arm of men will reap disappointment.

I have all this at the back of my mind even as I enter into partnership with people. I prepare well in advance for disappointment. I deliberately put in place checks and balances to help such partners fulfill their own side of the bargain.

Notwithstanding, I prepare my mind just in case because you never can say with man.

Marriage is one area where we just have to learn to forgive in advance. Marriage is supposed to be milk and honey but that has proven to be so only in theory and novels. In real life, marriage for many has become boxing arenas and a play ground for bitterness and not forgiving.

This should not be so. We must not count offense against us especially in marriage.

We should come to the marriage table with the heart of forgiveness. Not only that we must come prepared to say sorry even when we think we are right. We

must be like salt: salt as earlier said,
neither hears nor smell a thing.

Life is too short for anger and sadness.

QUOTE

"HAPPINESS IS WHEN WHAT YOU THINK, WHAT YOU SAY, AND WHAT YOU DO ARE IN HARMONY."

<u>MAHATMA GANDHI</u>

CHAPTER NINE

TEN MAJOR THINGS YOU CAN DO TO BOOST YOUR HAPPINESS

I will like to summarize this teaching by highlighting ten things that you can do to boost your own happiness:

1. **Accept the fact that nothing can ever be enough.** Money can never be enough even those who

have thousands are looking for millions while those who have millions are looking for billions. Nothing is ever enough under the sun. That is why we are told in the bible book of Proverbs that when wealth increases those that will eat it will also increase!

The moment you have money, the people will remember that you are related to them. That is when all the people remember that they can do one thing or the other for you. Then, all the people begin to approach you to buy even things you will not use in the next hundred years!

As a wise man you will only purchase or run after those things that you need not the things you want all the things people try to foist on you.

2. BE GRATEFUL FOR
   EVERYTHING YOU HAVE.

One of the things that give happiness is when you are contented with what you have. Get greed to be removed from you. Remove also the spirit of competition and striving!

None of them brings happiness.

The above should not be an excuse for a man to be idle. At the same time while a man is putting in his best at work he should not overexert himself in search of contentment because contentment is a state of the mind. It has nothing to do with your material possession and all your take-home pay.

Rather, happiness comes from knowing that none of these things can give you happiness but the happiness comes from your own mind and your attitude towards the things you have and the things that happen around you and the people that come around you.

3. Like people: but trust no one if you want to be happy. Do not base your happiness on what a man can or cannot do. Only God can be trusted.

   Whilst relating with people make preparation for a time they can come up with disappointments either by error of omission or commission

4. Accept that money cannot buy joy. Never forget that money can buy a nice bed but it cannot buy sleep. Never forget that when you keep money on the table it cannot sweep the house for you. Never

forget that you cannot take money to bed. Never forget that no matter the amount of money you keep at home that money cannot get up one morning and greet you good morning sir. Never forget that no matter the amount of money that money cannot pray for you!

In simple words there is a limit to what money can do for you.

In fact there is a kind of money you will have you begin to attract kidnappers and thieves to yourself.

So your happiness should not be tied to the number of or amount of money that you have. Remain Godly contented!

I want to tell the story of a rich king who was always having trouble in his palace. I read it somewhere. Permit me to quote it even though I forget the name of the author.

One day the rich man took a stroll through the city. He found that a family that was so obviously happy and was full of laughter whereas himself with all his gold diamond and silver was always having sleepless nights and troubled days.

He learnt on that trip that money is not everything.

Therefore a wise man will not tie his happiness to money.

5. Do not use your diary to record people's offences because long after you have forgiven the people and forgotten about their misbehavior, your diary is still carrying it and reminding you of what you ought to have forgotten.

Do not be like them villagers who mark the wall when they are offended. Some people even go as far as naming their children and domestic animals with names that keep reminding them of offences.

The unfortunate thing is that whenever such names are called they remember and they get bitter all over again.

When you forgive, wipe the slate completely. Leave nothing on it to keep reminding you of the offence.

Do not say it is impossible to do for it is very possible.

6. Happiness is a choice. Choose this day to live a life of joy. Decide that from this day going forward nothing can rock your boat. Decide that nothing can shake your cabinet. Decide to always look to the positive side and learn the lessons there in for a better you.

7. The company you keep matters a lot. If you want to be happy in life

you have to choose people who are positive minded to befriend.

Avoid people who never see anything good in others. Avoid people who are always complaining about this and that. Life is full of all stress. In fact, too much stress for you to take on all the stresses in and around other people to stress yourself some more!

Do not forget that they say tell me with whom you go and I will tell you what you are.

Evil communication corrupt good manners: Therefore mind the company you keep.

8.   In the same way you should listen to the right type of conversations. You should also be very mindful of the type of videos and tapes you listen to.

As a preacher myself I take pains to avoid certain videos. I live in a country where videos of Christian persecution, kidnappings, ritual killings and so on and so forth are circulated on a daily basis. Some of these videos are so gory and bbloody that I find it difficult to watch.

Since I do not want anything to make me sad unnecessarily, I mind what I watch. I avoid Boko Harmm videos and other videos with high violence.

I read books purely on recommendation just like a minister of the gospel should avoid things like pornographic films and erotica books.

Your happiness is so important that you need to be choosy of both your company and the things you hear or read.

9.   Most times we allow things happening around us to make us sad because we do not appreciate the protection of God.

If you want to really appreciate God more than you have ever done before, there is a very simple thing you can do. Get up for instance and go to visit the hospitals and prison yards.

There you will see a lot of people in crutches and in chains. You will see people who have lost their freedom and their health. You will see people who due to no fault of theirs, are victims of injustice and human errors.

Some have food but cannot eat while some can eat but they have no food.

Some of them have been in those situations for upwards of a year or two but here you are in full health and nothing evil happened to you.

You should be grateful to God. You may not have everything in life but you have your freedom and you have your good health.

Remember that as a human being, you are not in any way better than those who are gone. God in his mercy has preserved your life!

Therefore, you have reason to be grateful and thankful and not sorrowful in any way. Do not make yourself sad when you should be rejoicing!

10. One thing that is a healing balm that removes every form of bitterness from somebody is the word of God as contained in the Bible.

If you have not been studying it, I recommend that you add it to the books that you do read. If you really want to enjoy peace I suggest that you do more than reading it! Actually I recommend that you study, digest and apply the word in everything you do on Earth.

For every challenge that a man has faced or is likely to face, the word of God is complete and speaks to every situation and circumstance on Earth.

That's why Apostle Paul said to Timothy that he should study to show himself approved rightly dividing the word of Truth.

Also, in the book of Joshua we see God himself speaking to the young man that was leading Israel into the Promised Land telling him that for him to survive and be happy in the new place he was going, this book of the law must not depart from his mouth. You must study it and meditate upon it day and night.

When you meditate upon the word of God, it gives you peace and also wisdom that you need to navigate the difficulties and challenges of this world.

Whenever something troubles you, pick up the scriptures and study them then you will find peace.

11. It is good to read the Bible but you should not read it like a novel. You need the Holy Spirit to divinely open your eyes so that you can get the full meaning of the word of God.

If you are reading this now and you have not accepted Jesus Christ as your personal Lord and Savior, I entreat you to please set this book aside, go on your knees and plead with Christ to come into your life right now. Do this right now please.

After that Christ has come into your life, you ask for an in filling of the Holy Spirit.

When the Holy Spirit is in your life, he is a great Teacher and Comforter. He comes in to educate you concerning the confusing things of this world and to tell you what to do at a particular time.

He comes in to intercede for me and you in times of difficulty and to guide our feet from pits dug by our enemies.

Once you have brought Jesus Christ and the Holy Spirit into your life, ensure that you study the Bible regularly so that you can find the appropriate word to give you peace at all times and in all situations.

By so doing you will have enduring peace and happiness in your life.

"There is only one way to happiness and that is to cease worrying about things which are beyond the power of our will."

<u>Epictetus</u>

THANKS FOR READING THROUGH.

SHOULD YOU HAVE A NEED FOR PRAYERS, PLEASE EMAIL ME AT;
newochei@gmail.com

I ALSO ENCOURAGE YOU TO REACH ME WITH SUGGESTIONS YOU HAVE FOR THE IMPROVEMENT OF THIS BOOK IN THE NEXT EDITION.YOU CAN ALSO LEAVE AN HONEST REVIEW ON AMAZON.

ONCE MORE I THANK YOU FOR CHOOSING TO READ THIS BOOK AND I PRAY THAT ONE WORD REMAINS IN YOU LIFE FROM THIS LITTLE BOOK.

OTHER BOOKS BY THE SAME AUTHOR

1. HOW TO DEAL RUTHLESSLY WITH THE SPIRIT OF CONSPIRACY.
2. HOW TO DEAL RUTHLESSLY WITH SIN.
3. HOW TO DEAL RUTHLESSLY WITH USE AND DUMP SPIRIT.
4. HOW TO DEAL RUTHLESSLY WITH HATRED AND RACISM.
5. SO YOU CALL YOURSELF A PASTOR?
6. SO YOU CALL YOURSELF A MANAGER?
7. SO YOU CALL YOURSELF A HUSBAND?
8. HOW TO COUNSEL A MAD MAN

ABOUT THE AUTHOR

BISHOP OCHEI INNNOCENT, 64, IS THE PRESIDENT OF NEW DIMENSION SEMINARIES INTERNATIONAL.

HE IS A MEMBER OF THE INTERNATIONAL FELLOWSHIP OF THE CHRISTIAN CRISIS CENTERS, USA.

HE IS MARRIED TO LIZZY AND THEY ARE BLESSED WITH FOUR GOD FEARING CHILDREN

HE HAS BEEN IN MINISTRY FOR THREE DECADES AND IT HAS BEEN NOTHING BUT A FAITH WALK.

ABOUT THE BOOK

THE HUSTLE AND BUSTLE OF LIFE SEEM TO HAVE EATEN AWAY OUR FAMILY MORNING DEVOTIONS. WHERE IT STILL EXISTS, IT COMES ONCE A WHILE.

MANY OF OUR CHILDREN HAVE LOST INTEREST. THEY ARE NOT TOTALLY TO BLAME BECAUSE MANY DO NOT KNOW WHY SUCH EARLY MORNING PRAYERS ARE IMPORTANT!

THIS BOOK DETAILS THE IMPORTANCE OF MORNING FAMILY DEVOTIONS AND HIGHLIGHTS THE HINDRANCES SO THAT WE CAN BE MORE WARY.

IT IS AN IDEAL GIFT TO THE
YOUTH OF TODAY WHO NEEDS
TO KNOW WHY WE DO CERTAIN
THINGS AND NOT JUST BE
FORCED TO ACCEPT WHAT THEY
DO NOT UNDERSTAND.

NOTES

NOTES